THE TIDY GUIDE TO SELF-EDITING YOUR NOVEL

The clutter-free, 30-minute course for polishing your book without going crazy

---

RACHEL AUKES

.

WAYPOINT BOOKS

The Tidy Guide Series by Rachel Aukes

The Tidy Guide to Writing a Novel

The Tidy Guide to Self-Editing Your Novel

Coming 2019:

The Tidy Guide to Publishing a Novel

WAYPOINT BOOKS

THE TIDY GUIDE TO SELF-EDITING YOUR NOVEL

Please consider leaving a review wherever you bought the book, or
telling your friends about it, to help spread the word. Thank you for
supporting the author's work.

Cover Design by Evernight Designs.

Print ISBN-13: 978-1-7328449-2-6

Introduction

You've written a novel. This is a huge accomplishment, and you should be very proud. Far less than one percent of the world's population achieves this milestone. You may feel excited to proceed with the publishing process, but don't send your masterpiece to an editor—or click "publish" on Amazon—quite yet.

The digital age has brought us e-books and opened new publishing opportunities. But with over one million books published every year, your novel needs to stand out from the rest to get the attention it deserves. First impressions matter.

If you want to sell your novel to a publishing house, editors know that a polished manuscript is a sign of a professional author. (Note: A manuscript is a draft of a novel before it travels through the publishing process and becomes a book.) And when editors have dozens, sometimes hundreds, of manuscripts waiting in their slush piles, they may reject a story simply because it's hidden under typos.

Self-editing is important in traditional publishing, but

it's *crucial* in self-publishing. When you self-publish, you incur all the up-front costs in the publishing process, including cover design, interior formatting, and editing. The better you self-edit up front means the less work editors have to spend on your story, saving them time, which means the less they'll charge you for their services. Another bonus: The editing process won't seem nearly as overwhelming after you've gone through your story on your own, from an editorial perspective. And you'll discover that you'll become a better writer by broadening your linguistics expertise.

In this Tidy Guide—just thirty minutes of reading—I'll give you three clutter-free steps to revising, fixing, and polishing your manuscript so you can confidently carry it to the next step in process, whether that is self-publishing or submitting to agents or editors. The steps need not take long, and you can apply them to any length of prose, from novels to short stories. You can spend one session to go through all three steps in a single day, or you can break out the steps into multiple sessions.

I'll also provide you a free sample you can change to build your own, reusable style sheet. You'll have all the tools necessary to hone your story into an even better product.

Embrace the adventure!

Why is self-editing so hard?

Self-editing isn't easy. You've labored over every sentence, paragraph, and page of your story, and it's challenging to change something you've worked on for so long. However, editing is essential to a story that readers crave to read. The evolution of a novel is much like how a knife is made. Like a blade is formed from steel, a story is formed from the writer's mind. Then, just as a blade is sharpened in order to excel at its purpose, the story is honed through edits and rewrites.

Simply put, editing helps a good story become a *great* story.

What exactly is editing?

"Editing" is a broad term used for various types of revisions made to a document. In its simplest definition, to edit a manuscript is to change it for the better. We often think of these changes as fixing grammar mistakes and typographical errors, but editing goes far beyond those corrections.

My debut novel was rough, but an acquisitions editor at a small press found promise in it and offered me a contract. My first editor taught me that editing was a process—a series of activities—rather than a single deliverable. It's easier to think about editing in how it's applied to fiction, where you'll most often see editing broken into three levels, or "passes," as the editor will take at least one pass through a manuscript during each level.

The first level of editing is called **developmental editing**, also known as **content editing**. Here, my editor looked at my novel as a "big picture" in terms of characters, plot, worldbuilding, pacing, and other end-to-end layers. Content edits are generally provided to the author via an edit letter, followed up with a meeting to ensure both the editor and the author are on the same page.

When I received my first edit letter, I was shocked, then angry. In that letter, my editor recommended I delete an entire chapter that added nothing to drive the plot forward —the same chapter I'd spent days crafting. As if that weren't enough, she pointed out how my protagonist often behaved out of character in dialogue. And she introduced me to the bugaboo of many new writers: Chapter One began in the wrong place. But I loved that first sentence!

My editor recommended that I not make any changes until after a night's rest. And sure enough, I looked at my manuscript the next morning with a fresh perspective and realized my editor had pointed out real problems in the story. I had first taken the edit letter as an attack against me when, in reality, it was an objective list of expert recommendations to improve my story. After that "ah-ha" moment, I made the revisions with vigor and returned the document to my editor, who sent it on to the second level of editing.

Copyediting, sometimes called **line editing**, is

where an editor steps through a document, line by line, fixing errors in grammar, style, word usage, spelling, and punctuation. My editor returned the "redlined" manuscript, which displayed the Track Changes and Comments features found within Microsoft Word. These corrections were much easier to make, and my confidence grew. Since I was a new writer, I had much to learn in style and word usage, and my editor performed two copyediting passes to ensure we caught everything.

By the time we'd finished copyedits, I believed my story was spotless. I learned just how wrong I was during the third and final level of editing called **proofreading**. This is what many new writers mistakenly believe is the entire editing process, but it's only the final, quickest pass. Proof-reading focuses purely on typos and errors, such as missing words, incorrect punctuation, and misspellings.

When I received the redlined, proofed document, I couldn't believe the number of corrections the proofreader had made. I'd gone through that manuscript several times on my own before going through it another three times with my editor. This was when I understood why my editor brought in someone new to proofread: Both my editor and I were too close to the story, and we'd begun to skim over individual punctuation marks, letters, and spaces—we'd become blind to the little things.

Even after a complete editing process, a few small errors still made it through into the published novel. No editor can promise perfection. With your name on the cover, it's in your best interests to have your book edited, so that when your novel goes on sale, your readers can become absorbed into your story without numerous errors pulling them away.

Edit your book with a critical eye through three editing rounds

Self-editing is handled much like the standard three-step editing process. You first look at the overall story before going deeper into the content. The reason for this is that you may add, remove, or change entire chapters or at least paragraphs in the first pass. If you start at the deepest level, fixing typos, some of that work will prove unnecessary if you delete a paragraph you recently proofread. Likewise, if you add new content after you've proofread, then parts of your manuscript will need re-proofed.

To save you time and energy, I recommend performing three, focused editing rounds, where you go through your manuscript three times, each time looking at things from a different perspective, and mirroring the three phases of editing traditionally performed on fiction.

In Round 1, you will take a step back to look at the story overall. Here, you will look at the **3Ps**: *plot*, *people*, and *pacing*. I'll give you shortcuts so you can confidently and quickly complete the first round.

In Round 2, you'll fix the story line by line. Here, you'll focus on the *style* you're using and common *snags* that pull readers out of the story. I'll give you a style sheet that you can personalize to make this step a breeze.

Last, in Round 3, you'll read your story out loud to make it shine. As a writer, you're likely an avid reader. And this step entails leveraging something you already love to do, and that's reading!

Round 1. Step back to see the big picture

"When your story is ready for rewrite, cut it to the bone. Get rid of every ounce of excess fat. This is going to hurt; revising a story down to the bare essentials is always a little like murdering children, but it must be done." ~ *Stephen King*

The first round of self-editing is to look at your overall story. Here, you'll focus on the major components of the story, paying no attention to individual words, or else you risk being distracted—in terms of a common expression, you won't see the forest through the trees.

While content editing performed by a developmental editor is much more immersive than what I propose, covering the 3Ps (*plot*, *people*, and *pacing*) will allow you to address the most common story problems quickly without making the first round feel like an overwhelming chore. Depending on what you find in your story, Round 1 can be the fastest or the most time-consuming of the three rounds of self-editing.

Keep the parts the story needs and drop the rest (Plot)

The first P activity, focused on your story's plot, will go much faster if you have a storyboard, as introduced in *The Tidy Guide to Writing a Novel*. Your storyboard lists all your story's scenes and plot points, including all twists and turns. If you don't have a storyboard, you must pull those plot points from your story as you review each scene within every chapter.

A scene is an event that takes place within your story, and a chapter may contain one or more scenes. The plot is the overall story thread, and each plot point is a place in your story where that thread veers in a new direction.

If you have a storyboard, you don't even need to look at your manuscript for this activity. Here's what you do ...

Make sure every scene is included in your storyboard. Don't miss any. The key to succeeding at plot is to understand every scene of your story. If you find your storyboard too detailed to pick out the scenes, write out each scene on its own notecard, using just enough words to make it clear what happens in that scene. For example, "Cash is attacked by her co-worker in the office bathroom" is the opening scene from *100 Days in Deadland*. Be sure not to skip any scenes, because you'll want to see each one clearly for this activity.

I use Post-it® notes to transcribe all the scenes from my storyboard so I can better see the flow of the story. I add stars next to turning points in the story. After I create each note, I stick it on my wall—scenes from a single novel often fill my entire wall.

Once you have a clear picture of each scene in your story, ask yourself the following two questions:

1. Will readers see any holes, contradictions, or lack of plausibility in the plot? If they can't suspend their disbelief, they can't become absorbed into your story. Skim through your scenes. Mark any places where you may need to add in more detail or make changes to ensure the plot is believable from beginning to end.

2. Are there any scenes that don't move the plot forward? Now, focus on your scenes. If you find a scene that has no tie to the plot, delete the scene. Your goal here is to leave out the parts that readers would skim over. Often, these are the infamous "day in the life" scenes. On my first book, I cut two entire chapters because they didn't move the story forward. Just because you cut the scene from your story doesn't mean it has to go in the garbage. Some scenes make excellent fodder for bonus features, short stories, or newsletter extras.

Once you've finished answering the two questions above, open your document. Make the changes needed to strengthen your story.

Reinforce your character traits (People)

Once you've addressed your story's plot, you're ready to move on to the second P activity, and that's looking at your story's people. For this exercise, you'll work within your manuscript.

Before you begin, make a list of all major characters within your story. This includes your protagonist, antagonist, and their key supporting cast. Skip minor characters who may appear in only a chapter or two. Your list will have the names of roughly two to ten characters, and you'll focus on each character at a time.

To begin, pick one of the character names. I often start at the bottom of my list—with a supporting character—because they are easier to scan and help you build momentum in completing this exercise (Little Ups!). Now, open your document. I'm assuming you have your manuscript in an electronic format, such as in Microsoft Word, which makes this activity a breeze. Search for all occurrences of that character's name, e.g., *Reyne*. This will highlight the character's name, making it easier to see everywhere the character appears in your story.

Skim through your document, looking only at this character, with the following questions in mind:

1. Do they have their own personality? Even a supporting character shouldn't feel like a cardboard cutout. Give each character unique traits and personality quirks to help them feel like a real person with whom readers can empathize.

2. Do they ever act out of character? Make sure your character is acting true to himself or herself rather than as a device to force your plot ahead in the direction you want. This is a big one, because readers will notice if the star of your story suddenly does something out of character.

3. Do they respond to stimuli with reaction beats? When something happens to the character, whether it's a physical, verbal, or psychological action, be sure to allow them to have a visceral reaction. Newton's third law, "for every reaction, there's an equal and opposite reaction," applies to characters as well as to motion. By ensuring your characters have reaction beats, you enrich their personality and individual depth.

As you step through your character within the story, take notes or make changes as you proceed. When you finish with the character, repeat the activity for the next character on your list. When you reach your protagonist, add one more question to your list:

4. Does the protagonist change throughout the

story? Nearly all stories are character-driven—they focus on things happening to the protagonist who must then respond and address the overall conflict. Just like in real life, when big things happen to us, we change in some way. Perhaps your character becomes wiser, more emotionally guarded, and gains an improved sense of self-worth. Or, your character develops new values, such as altruism, compassion, or leadership. Likely, you know how your protagonist evolves—be sure your readers see it, too, through your character's actions, words, and thoughts.

After you've finished reviewing your characters, you can move on to the third and final P activity.

If it sounds like writing, rewrite it (Pacing)

When you review your story's *pacing*—you'll also work within your manuscript. Open your document and perform the following steps:

1. Read the first three pages. Does the story begin at the right place? Does it grab the reader? With more and more books for readers to choose from, grabbing a reader's attention in the first page has become more important than ever. My first three books all began at the wrong place, and I ended up cutting the scenes (and my beautifully written first lines!) to drop the reader into action sooner. Be careful to not begin with your protagonist's deep point-of-view (POV), as readers have not yet had the time to fall in love with your character. Instead, give the reader stimuli to which they can watch the character(s) respond. If you're stuck, watch a movie in the same genre to see how it snags your attention within the first few minutes.

2. Read the final three pages. Is the plot (and subplot, if applicable) wrapped up? Will the reader feel satisfied? Try not to leave loose ends. Be careful with cliffhangers. If you have a cliffhanger, the novel's plot should still be resolved even if the overarching series plot is ongoing. Readers are fine with and enjoy an ongoing *series* plot, but that's different from your *story's* plot. If you leave the story's plot unresolved, you don't have a story—you have only a partial story.

3. Skim through the entire manuscript, looking at the balance of dialogue and narrative. There needs to be both action (fast-paced) and reaction (slower-paced) scenes. For this activity, don't read anything. Instead, you'll look at white space and the overall flow of your story. If you see multiple pages of dialogue, insert snippets of narrative, such as the protagonist's thoughts. Likewise, if you see multiple pages of long-paragraph narrative, break it up. The key is to have dialogue and narrative flow together through the story.

The extent of changes needed during the first pass of self-edits varies by story. Round 1 may take you only an hour, or it could take you a full day or more. There are no hard and fast rules here. The key is to find the big things that are most likely to cause a reader to leave a book unread. Once you complete the first round, you can confidently move onto the next round to fix your story's style and snags.

Round 2. Step in to fix line by line

In the second round of self-editing, you'll go through your manuscript line by line. Here, you'll focus on *style*, which refers to how grammar, words, and punctuation are used within a written work.

The English language is complicated, and its rules—and exceptions to its rules—can be headache-inducing. Fortunately, there are many tools to help streamline this round. Nearly all fiction editors today adhere to *The Chicago Manual of Style*, so you can't go wrong sticking with what readers expect. You can also use Word's search functionality to cut down the amount of energy spent on this editing activity.

Use a style sheet to save time

Before you begin, consider creating your own, personal **style sheet** that you can use to self-edit all your stories—not only the one you're currently writing, but also all future stories. There are hard-and-fast writing rules, such as which numbers should be spelled, but there are also rules, such as unique words, that you'll set for your own writing.

You'll use your style sheet as essentially a self-editing checklist to search-and-replace specific punctuation marks, words you tend to overuse, and so on. Since every writer has their own personal style and preferences, build your style sheet however it best works for you.

I've included in Appendix C a sample style sheet I've used. Use this as a start to building your own—as I've built it from working with several editors over a dozen novels and a couple dozen short stories. You can also download a sample style sheet off my website (www.RachelAukes.com/extras). For the industry standard style guide, the current edition of *The Chicago Manual of Style* contains every rule regarding style, usage, and grammar. The book is hefty, and it's offered in an online format (subscription required). For a simpler guide, see Strunk and White's *The Elements of Style*, which is a wonderful pocketbook reference.

You shouldn't attempt to recreate *The Chicago Manual of Style* in your personal style sheet. Rather, your style sheet should contain a list of reminders on how to handle certain types of words and punctuation marks, so you don't have to look up how to handle them every time you use them.

All professional editors are familiar with style guides and style sheets. If you share your personal style sheet with your editor, not only will you save them time, but they may also help you update it for future use. Trust me, you'll never regret having your own style sheet. Your personal writing style sheet will save you hours upon hours and will ensure consistency across multiple books, especially if those books fall within the same series.

If you'd like additional support to make things go even faster, there are third party software tools you can use, many of them with free options. I use ProWritingAid as a secondary check. Other software programs include Grammarly, Auto Crit, Hemingway Editor, and many more.

For an easy win (Little Up!) run Microsoft Word's spell and grammar checks, with the caveat to not trust everything they recommend. The checks are notorious for misidentifying correct grammar as much as identifying errors.

Whether you use a professional style guide, a personal style sheet, software tools, or all, you'll look at your story with an eye on two things: style and snags. While I've broken the pair out in this book, you can address both at the same time as you step through your manuscript.

To conduct this round of self-edits, open your document and have your personal style sheet as a reference at your side. Your style sheet should include all important details related to your writing style and common snags to fix. I explain the two categories below.

Review the sentences, words, and punctuation (Style)

I write in Microsoft Word and use its tools for much of my self-editing. When I review my manuscript for consistency, I use the *Search* (or *Find*) feature often to search for a particular word for punctuation mark. That way, I can focus on a specific item, such as an ellipsis or exclamation point, and see how it's used throughout the story. I treat each category in my style sheet as a checklist item to speed up my self-editing process.

Below are five of the most common categories you might include in your personal style sheet to speed up your self-editing session. See Appendix C for a comprehensive list.

- **Word usage** refers to using the correct word, e.g., *lay* or *lie*. I overuse *it*, so I include an item in my style sheet to search for "it" in my document to make sure that anytime I use that word, the meaning is clear.
- **Dialogue tags** show who's speaking and can show changes in emotion. *Said* is generally the best tag, and you certainly want to avoid impossible tags. For example, someone can't *laugh* a statement, but they can say something *with* a laugh.
- **Punctuation marks.** Exclamation points denote strong emotions, such as shouting, and they stand out when they're overused (and are often a red flag of a writer telling a story and not showing it). I once quit reading a series I otherwise enjoyed, simply because the exclamation points exhausted me to the point that I set down the book and never returned. An editor once recommended to have no more than one exclamation point to every one hundred pages. Now, I won't prescribe any rules, but if you have an exclamation point on every page, do a search and see how many of those instances are truly instances of strong emotions. If they're not, then change that exclamation point to a period.
- **Comma.** The serial comma, also known as the Oxford comma, is the industry standard for novels, but there is some flexibility for personal preference as long as you're consistent.
- **Capitalization.** Indicate what should be capitalized and what shouldn't. E.g., family terms aren't capitalized (e.g., *I love my mother.*),

but those terms used as names are capitalized (e.g., *I love Mother*.). Since I write science fiction, my style sheet includes a note to capitalize names of planets and asteroids.

Things to keep out of your novel (Snags)

Snags are devilish words and descriptions that can hurt the reader's experience and are common mistakes of new writers. As you step through your manuscript, look to cut:

- **Purple prose**, which is flowery, overdrawn descriptions and dramatic dialogue. To the reader, this comes across like the author is trying too hard.
- **Information dumps.** This is a classic case of telling the reader instead of showing them. Say only what's necessary and sprinkle in details later, or blend the information in dialogue and narrative.
- **RUE,** which stands for **Resist the Urge to Explain**. When you explain things, you're telling the reader what's happening. Let the reader experience it instead.

To save time, you can search your document for certain words that may take away from the reader's experience. These are the top three types of words to cut or replace:

- **Filter words**, also known as **telling words**. These words are generic and distance the reader from the protagonist's experience. Examples of these words are *saw, looked, heard, felt, noticed, knew, watched, smelled,* and *tasted.*

- **Adverbs.** While adverbs aren't inherently bad, they are often overused, especially in dialog tags (e.g., … *she said frantically*). Search for "ly" in your document to catch many of the most common adverbs (e.g., *nearly, barely, only*) and see if you can't replace the adverb with a stronger verb.
- **Garbage words.** These words are rarely needed and often weaken the story. Examples of these words include *really, very, so, just, good/great,* and *quite.* Delete them, and chances are, your story will be all the better.

Round 3. Read aloud to make your story shine

Polish your novel until it shines

You've made it to the final round of self-edits. This is by far the easiest of the three rounds but not always the fastest. Here, you'll proofread your manuscript to catch any remaining typos; repetitive words or sentence structure; and incorrect, duplicate, or missing words.

To proofread, find a comfortable chair and read the story out loud to yourself. Or if you prefer, have your computer, Alexa, or Siri read your story to you. Reading aloud provides two benefits: first, it forces you to slow down and see every word; and second, your ears pick up the story's rhythm and you'll hear awkward lines.

When you catch words or sentences you need to change, you can either change it on the spot or mark the page and continue reading. I do the latter when I read aloud, so I don't lose momentum.

After you finish reading and making corrections, be sure to celebrate the milestone. Self-editing can be a mentally exhausting but very rewarding process. You can now say your manuscript is as polished as it can be to your ability.

Congratulations!

What comes after self-editing

Critique partners are your allies

As an optional step, you may want someone you trust to read the manuscript before you enter it into the publishing process. For many writers, this person is a **critique partner**.

A critique partner is a writer who can offer a fresh perspective on your story. Many writer organizations and writing groups can help you find a partner, but keep in mind that not all critique partners are equal. A good critique partner will give suggestions on how to improve *your* story, not how *they* would handle a particular scene. A good critique partner is a precious resource for no cost— but be sure to return the favor by being their critique partner, too.

Beta readers can also provide valuable opinions, especially in terms of the 3Ps. Beta readers are readers who love to help out their favorite authors. If this is your first book, you'll have a far easier time finding critique partners than beta readers. As you publish books, readers will come to you, begging to get involved. Having beta readers is like having a finger on the pulse of your readership. You'll hear what works (and what doesn't) for them. With beta readers, you'll receive a wealth of feedback, but be careful to retain ownership of your story as you envision it. You can't and shouldn't try to please everyone.

If you work with a critique partner or beta readers, consider each piece of feedback you receive, but you certainly aren't expected to incorporate every piece in your story. Sometimes, a simple rephrasing of a sentence is all it takes to address a reader's comment that they didn't understand something.

I've seen a few writers take the feedback personally. They've grown so attached to their story that they don't want to cut a single word. I can understand—those words took a lot of time and energy to write. The key is to remember that any feedback reflects the story, not the author. No story is perfect. It doesn't matter if you're J. K. Rowling, Stephen King, or a first-time novelist, everyone's story needs edited.

Refine your personal style sheet

If you've sent your manuscript to a critique partner, now is a great time to update your style sheet. Even after over a dozen published novels, I continue to tweak my personal style sheet after every self-editing marathon. Often, there's a particular word or a punctuation item I always seem to get wrong. Updating your style sheet takes only a couple of minutes, but it'll save you hours when you go to self-edit your next story.

Enter the publishing process

You've done it! You've written and polished a story that's ready for the publishing process. You must now decide which publishing approach is best for your novel, whether that's traditional publishing, self-publishing, or something in between the two models.

There are pros and cons to each publishing path you choose. Traditional publishing often offers an up-front advance and guides you through the publishing process, but it can also be frustratingly slow—from finding an agent or editor through release often takes longer than a year.

Self-publishing can be much faster. You have complete control over every aspect of the process, but that means you bear full responsibility for every aspect and incur some upfront costs for cover design and editing.

In my upcoming *The Tidy Guide to Publishing Your Novel,* I cover the complete processes involved with your publishing options and step-by-step how to proceed into the publishing journey.

You'll continue to learn and improve with every story

Self-editing can be hard work and will test your humility. But it can also be highly rewarding as you see your story morph into an even better version. Your confidence and skills grow as you test your writing and analytical knowledge. You may even find yourself excited to write your next book!

Appendix A. Storyboard for Fringe Runner

This storyboard is available to download in notecard format at www.RachelAukes.com/extras.

Chapter 1: *The Package*
Scene 1: Reyne retrieves a package from a dead Myrad ship in the direct path of a star swarm (setting: space)

Chapter 2: *A Ship Caught in the Swarm*
Scene 2: Reyne escapes with the package and returns to the Gryphon (setting: space, on board the Gryphon)
Scene 3: The Gryphon is force-docked by a CUF warship (setting: space, on board the Arcadia)

Chapter 3: *Collective Cages*
Scene 4: Reyne's crew is detained (setting: space, on board the Arcadia)
Scene 5: Heid has Reyne's package seized while she probes his past (setting: space, on board the Arcadia)

Chapter 4: *Unfinished Business*

Scene 15: The Gryphon reaches Sol Base to discover it's been hit by the blight (setting: space, on board the Gryphon)

Chapter 12: *Deadly Pursuits*
Scene 16: The Gryphon escapes the CUF and flees to Ice Port (setting: space, on board the Gryphon)

Chapter 13: *Toxic Complications*
Scene 17: Heid learns the blight was released at Sol Base on Darios (setting: space, on board the Arcadia)

Chapter 14: *Haunted Visions*
Scene 18: The Gryphon lands on Playa (setting: Tulan Base)
Scene 19: The CUF Trinity attacks Ice Port (setting: viewed from Tulan Base)

Chapter 15: *Frozen Sorrow*
Scene 20: As Ice Port is destroyed, Reyne's crew figure out their next steps (setting: Tulan Base)

Chapter 16: *Truth in Words*
Scene 21: Critch arrives in the Honorless; Reyne and Critch reach an uneasy partnership (setting: Tulan Base)

Chapter 17: *Faded Liaisons*
Scene 22: Heid receives an invitation from the Seamstress (setting: space, on board the Arcadia)

Chapter 18: *Distant Dreams*
Scene 23: The Honorless and Gryphon depart Ice Port to meet Heid (setting: Tulan Base)

Chapter 27: *Corrupted Illusions*
Scene 34: Critch and Reyne travel to meet the Mason, who betrays them; the traitor is revealed; a crew member is killed (setting: Alluvia warehouse)

Chapter 28: *Staring into the Abyss*
Scene 35: Heid learns she was betrayed by Sebin (setting: space, on board the Arcadia)
Scene 36: Heid kills Sebin (setting: space, on board the Arcadia)

Chapter 29: *The Stuff of Nightmares*
Scene 37: Reyne, Critch, and crew escape Mason's trap and the CUF by entering Alluvia's monster-infested waters (setting: Alluvia)
Scene 38: Throttle rescues Reyne, Critch, and crew (setting: Alluvia space docks)

Chapter 30: *The Uprising*
Scene 39: Critch transmits files to all the fringe, revealing the truth of the blight; Reyne and Critch finally make amends (setting: Nova Colony)

Appendix B. Self-Editing Checklist

This checklist is available to download at www.RachelAukes.com/extras.

Round 1: Step back to see the big picture (plot, people, and pacing)

Plot

- Review your storyboard.

People

- Review each character, with special attention on the protagonist.

Pacing

- Read the beginning.
- Read the ending.
- Skim everything in between.

Round 2: Step in to fix line by line (style and snags)

Style

- Run a spelling and grammar program.
- Review your grammar, word usage, punctuation, and unique terms.

Snags

- Cut words and descriptions that can hurt the reader's experience.

Round 3: Proofread to make your story shine

- Read your manuscript aloud.

Wrap-Up

- Make sure the formatting is consistent and correct.
- Save a backup copy of your manuscript.
- Update your personal style sheet.

Appendix C. Sample Personal Style Sheet

This sample is available to download at www.RachelAukes.com/extras.

Use this style sheet as a starter to build your own style sheet. Your style sheet should contain word usage and punctuation rules that you may forget or apply inconsistently, as well as unique terms and custom usage of words and styles that you use within your fiction.

General Tips

- Main reference materials: *The Chicago Manual of Style*, Strunk and White's *The Elements of Style*, *Merriam-Webster Dictionary* (unabridged-Web).
- Run spell and grammar checks in Microsoft Word.
- Run third-party grammar program.

Formatting

- Chapter headings should be *Heading 1* style.
- Body text should be *Normal* style.
- Section breaks are three asterisks ******* with one line before and after.

Word Usage Rules and Tips

- Use dialogue tags to show who's speaking and changes in emotion. When in doubt, *said* is the best tag. Avoid impossible tags. E.g., *"Never," he hissed*.
- Make sure antecedents are clear (e.g., *he, she, it*). Avoid using the word *it* when possible.
- Use the correct word. E.g., *okay, not OK; its vs. it's, lay vs. lie*.
- Use *who* for humans and named animals, such as pets. Use *that* for inanimate objects and unnamed animals.
- Do not put direct thoughts in italics. E.g., *Jasmine will get her comeuppance, he thought.*
- Use the possessive *s* in all names except names ending in a "z" or "z" sound. E.g., *Marcus's dog, Topaz' cat.*
- Replace clichés in narrative with fresh, new descriptors. (Clichés are okay in dialogue.)
- Avoid roaming body parts. E.g., *Her eyes flew to the man as he entered the room.*
- Avoid purple prose. Cut flowery language, overdrawn descriptions, and overly dramatic dialogue.

- Resist the Urge to Explain (RUE). Trust the reader's intelligence.
- Replace or cut garbage words. E.g., *really, very, so, that, just, good, well, quite.*
- Replace filter words (i.e., telling words) with better descriptors. E.g., *looked, heard, felt, thought, noticed, watched, knew.*
- Replace adverbs (think *-ly*) with stronger verbs when possible. E.g., *loudly, nearly, there, near, once, soon.* Tip: Adverbs are descriptors that tell how, how often, when, and where.
- Replace adjectives with stronger nouns.
- Cut overused words. E.g., *that, s/he, just, like, and, but, as, then.*
- Avoid generic descriptions. E.g., *the man.*
- Choose interesting linking verbs when possible to replace *is, was, were, of the, to be.*
- Minimize similes.
- Avoid obscure words that require readers to leave the story and consult a dictionary.
- Keep a list of unique terms (or unique usage of words) used. E.g., *planetside, dromuulier, Playa, Playans.*

Punctuation Rules

Periods

- Use only single spaces after periods. *Tip: Search and replace all double spaces in manuscript with single spaces.*

Quotations

- Avoid using single quotes (' ') outside quotation marks. In North America, they should never be outside quotations (" ").
- Minimize the use of quotation marks or italics for emphasis or to show sarcasm.

Ellipses

- Use a space before and after three points (...), E.g., *She didn't seem so bad ... for a citizen.*
- Search and replace three periods with the ellipsis symbol.
- Note: If not using Word's ellipsis symbol, put a space between each dot.

Comma

- Use the serial comma (aka Oxford or Harvard comma), i.e., put commas between the last two items in a list. E.g., *He bought milk, eggs, and bread.*
- No comma is needed to separate short independent clauses. E.g., *She had him cornered and he knew it.*
- No comma is needed after a conjunction when it begins a sentence. E.g., *And she ran.*
- Use a comma before a proper name, nickname, or title in dialogue. E.g., *"I don't care, pal."*

Hyphens

- In general, don't hyphenate compound nouns. E.g., *She leaned against the armrest.*
- In general, hyphenate compound adjectives. E.g., *Critch swallowed the up-front costs.*

- When in doubt, refer to a dictionary.
- Keep a list of unique terms that should (or shouldn't) be hyphenated. E.g., *g-force, firsthand.*

Em Dash and En Dash

- An em dash is an interruption in a sentence. Don't use a space before or after. E.g., *"What brings you here—wait, let me guess —the cash."*
- If an em dash interrupts a statement, exclude the punctuation mark. *E.g., What the—*
- Use an en dash in place of *to* between two open compounds. E.g., *1931–1935, pages 1–5.*

Capitalization

- Capitalize family terms only when used as a name. E.g., *Mom refused to listen. My mom hugged me.*
- Capitalize formal titles. E.g., *President Jones remained at the White House. The Queen of England smiled. Yes, Captain.* Don't capitalize general titles. E.g., *The president and the queen laughed. The captain took control.*
- Capitalize the first letter after a colon only if the clause is a full sentence. E.g., *I told you before: You must do exactly as I say. This is what I want: a monkey in a barrel.*
- Capitalize nicknames when they take the place of names. E.g., *Jan and Spike headed out.*
- Don't capitalize terms of endearment or respect. E.g., *honey, babe, sir, ma'am.*
- Use all CAPS only when shouting or showing a

sign written in that style. E.g., *He read the sign.*
GO AWAY.

Numbers

- Spell out numbers one through ninety-nine.
  Hyphenate mixed numbers. E.g., *ten, thirty-four.*
- Spell out whole numbers over one hundred.
  E.g., *He fired a thousand rounds and still faced*
  overwhelming odds.
- Use numerals for mixed numbers over one
  hundred. E.g., *She could count 356 reasons why she*
  should turn around and leave.
- Spell out numbers that begin a sentence. E.g.,
  Two hundred and two days later, she returned home.
- Percentages (%) are spelled out. E.g., *Sam was*
  ninety-nine percent sure Dave cheated him.
- Use numerals for years. E.g., *1921.*
- Use Roman numerals for wars, monarchs, and
  popes. *E.g., World War III, King William II.*

Also by Rachel Aukes

The Tidy Guides Series (Nonfiction)

The Tidy Guide to Writing a Novel

The Tidy Guide to Self-Editing Your Novel

Fringe Series

Fringe Runner

Fringe Station

Fringe Campaign

Fringe War

Fringe Legacy

Colliding Worlds Trilogy

Collision

Implosion

Explosion

The Deadland Saga

100 Days in Deadland

Deadland's Harvest

Deadland Rising

Standalone Fiction

Stealing Fate

About the Author

Rachel Aukes is the award-winning author of *100 Days in Deadland*, which made Suspense Magazine's Best of the Year list. She is also a Wattpad Star, her stories having over five million reads. When not writing, she can be found flying old airplanes across the Midwest countryside and catering to an exceptionally spoiled fifty-pound lapdog.

Join Rachel's readers club to get early access to new releases, sign up for contests, and receive free stuff: www.rachelaukes.com/newsletter